HIRE GREAT PEOPLE

By the author

How To Shine

Peak Performance Every Time

Two Lengths Of The Pool

Could I Do That?

How To Herd Cats

Stronger Together

How To Develop Character

Master Mental Toughness

Silence Your Demons

HIRE
GREAT
PEOPLE

SIMON HARTLEY

First published in Great Britain in 2022 by Be World Class.

Copyright © Simon Hartley 2022

The moral right of the author has been asserted.

All rights reserved.

No part of this publication may be reproduced, stored in a retrieval system or transmitted in any form or by any means, without the prior permission in writing of the publisher, nor be otherwise circulated in any form of binding or cover other than that in which it is published and without similar conditions including this condition being imposed on the subsequent purchaser.

A CIP catalogue record of this book is available from the British Library.

ISBN 978-1-3999-5407-5

Typeset in EB Garamond by Louise Carrier.

Printed and bound in Great Britain.

Be World Class Ltd

Lister House

Lister Hill

Leeds

LS18 5DZ

be-world-class.com

ACKNOWLEDGMENTS

Writing a book is a team sport!

I could not have written this without the help of a few fantastic people.

Firstly, my wonderful wife and daughters who
support me in everything I do.

I'd also like to say a huge thank you to James Roach for writing
the Foreword, and his passion for recruiting on character.

And, last but by no means least, the amazing Louise
Carrier for her brilliant cover design, illustrations,
typesetting and support with publication.

PREFACE

I am not a recruitment consultant.

I have no background in recruitment whatsoever.

So, what qualifies me to write a book about how to hire great people?

My background is sport psychology - helping elite athletes and sports teams to win championships and break records.

My real passion, interest and curiosity has always been to work with and study the very best in the world. I want to know how they're different. What do they do that others don't do... or won't do? How do they think? How do they approach challenges?

I don't do this purely because it's interesting and enjoyable (although it is both!). I do it so that we can learn from them and adopt the principles that make them great.

Over the last 25 years or so, I've seen dozens of truly world-class teams and organisations at work – from elite special forces units to chefs in Michelin-starred kitchens, world-championship-winning sports teams, surgical teams and world-leading aerobatic display teams. I've studied what they do. And I've noticed something...

They recruit very differently to most!

I've heard loads of leaders say, "We want to hire on attitude and train skills." And I know they have every intention of doing it.

But the problem is... they don't really know how.

World-class organisations have figured it out. They want to hire on character AND they've found a way to do it!

Throughout the course of this short book, I'll lift the lid on what they do. I'll share the common principles that these amazing organisations adopt. I'll also share the methods that I've used with my clients in elite sport, business, education, healthcare, and the military. And we'll explore how you can apply these same approaches in your own organisation.

FOREWORD

---

by James Roach,
Managing Director of Headstar.

I'm fortunate to have had two careers so far – the first in finance and the second in recruitment. I like working with numbers and I like working with people so you can imagine, that in the form of running Headstar, a finance recruitment consultancy, I've found my utopia.

What my time in finance taught me is that you can put a number on anything and find out whether it's working or not. In recruitment it's no different; it's simply how many of your hires were a success as a percentage of your total hires. There are countless metrics that we analyse in business and for some reason recruitment isn't one, yet it's a vitally important indicator of the business's success or failure. How often do we see or hear business leaders talking about the importance of hiring great people? Yet whenever I ask them what their success rate is, they only have a "rough idea." Ask them what their margin is or year-on-year sales growth, and it rolls off the tongue almost instantly. If we're honest about being really good at hiring, then we need to start measuring how good we are:

Recruitment success rate = successful hires as a % of total hires.

I saw Simon's presentation *"Hiring on Character"* in 2018 alongside my Chairman at the time. We had our mouths open for the majority of the session, probably because it was so blindingly obvious, yet we'd done nothing to change our archaic way of hiring people. We contacted Simon the following day and spent the following six months devising a process to hire people on character. He helped us dissect the character traits of our top performers and to set about forming a rigorous process to spot and test these traits in our future hires. It was arduous; it was hard work, and it challenged all of our beliefs about recruitment. But the results speak for themselves.

At the time of writing, we're seven years into our business journey, with the first two years of our hiring being 'normal' and the last five years being 'on character'.

In the first two years we recruited eleven people, six of whom didn't work out (Recruitment success rate = 45%).

In the following five years we've recruited eighteen people, two of whom didn't work out (Recruitment success rate = 89%).

Headstar Recruitment Success Rate

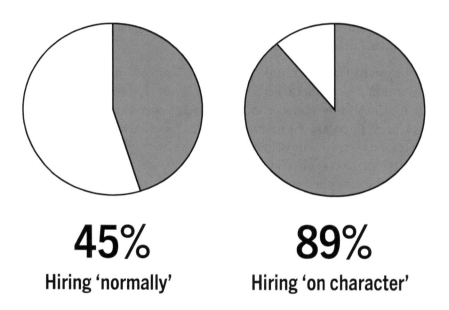

45%
Hiring 'normally'

89%
Hiring 'on character'

My Chairman and I had been in business for a number of years. We'd both been hiring people since early in our respective careers and quite frankly 'fancied ourselves' as pretty good at it. You know the drill – we followed our gut, went with people we could have a beer with, that kind of thing...I cringe these days as I look back at how we conducted ourselves.

Speaking from experience, and with the evidence to prove it, we found that Simon's process not only works but it changes the whole culture of the business. New recruits are welcomed with open arms in a show of "you made it through, well done!" The team know that they've been recruited because of their match with our desired character traits, and there's a pride associated with that. Trust has also been built up; no longer is it a case of "wonder who management are going to hire this time?!" but instead the team are excited to meet the newest member of this elite 'club' and trust that we've done a great job of testing them first.

Problem is, I'm now enormously frustrated. Mostly with our clients. I think we're brilliant at presenting a great talent pool to businesses. We then rely on the business to appoint who they think is the best candidate, but they don't always do that. And they come back to us asking for another talent pool and the process starts again (and we're often blamed for this!). So, we want to muscle our way into the process a bit more. We see too many businesses that don't know how to recruit great people that fit their culture brilliantly. That's why I gleefully agreed to write this foreword for Simon. I'd like for nothing less than the entire business community to read this book cover to cover and apply all of the lessons to their hiring process. I'd encourage them to throw caution to the wind and forget what they think they know about hiring (as well as how good they think they are at it).

I'm going to ask Simon for a truckload of copies (hopefully for free, doubt it though…) and slip one into the in-trays of MDs around the country. Let's get our recruitment success rate percentages in board packs worldwide and start recognising the need to do as the Red Arrows do if we want to hire great team players. Thank you, Simon, for studying and introducing this concept to us. To everyone reading, I sincerely hope it has the same impact on you as it did on us.

CONTENTS

———

INTRODUCTION

We all hire people.

Even solo entrepreneurs hire people. They may not employ them. They may not add them to their payroll or organisational chart... but they still recruit people. In our business, Be World Class, we have two employees – myself and my wife. We've only ever had two employees. But, over the years, we've recruited hundreds of people. We hire suppliers, such as web designers, graphic designers, video editors, book editors, accountants and so on. We recruit partners, particularly for events and joint ventures. I also recruit clients (although I wouldn't say I 'hire' them).

And, whether they're employees, suppliers, partners, or clients, I always want to work with truly great people!

In my experience, it makes a HUGE difference!!

But what difference does it make to you?

What's the difference between hiring great people and average people... or below average people?

What's the cost of getting it wrong?

How much time, effort and energy do you lose?

What impact does it have on your team and culture?

Is there a reputational cost?

What's the financial cost – in recruitment fees, lost revenue, salary, etc?

What's the upside when you get it right?

How much is a great person worth, compared to an average person?

How much more productive are they?

How much more income or profit do they generate?

What's their impact on the team?

What's their impact on client relationships or your reputation?

These are questions that are worth spending a few minutes on. It's also worth thinking of specific people you've recruited in the past – those who were 'great' and those who were 'below average' – to reflect on the impact they had.

I asked these same questions to a Sales Director once. He described his recruitment as, "Hit and miss, but with less hits and more misses." Over the years he'd hired dozens of sales executives, most of whom didn't make the grade.

As he answered these questions, he started to calculate the financial cost of getting it wrong. There was normally a recruitment fee, paid to a recruitment agency. Then there was the salary paid to these sales executives, who typically stayed with the business six to nine months before they finally parted company. He also talked about the cost of training as well as the time that his team invested into the whole recruitment, induction, and training process. And, despite all their investment, many of these sales executives delivered zero (or minimal) sales.

He told me that, conservatively, each bad hire would cost them £25,000 but it could be closer to £50,000.

I also asked him about the benefits of hiring a really good sales executive. If we compared a really good sales executive with an average one, how much extra revenue would the good sales executive bring in?

He said, "At least £150,000 extra per year... minimum... but it could easily be double that."

So, in his world, the difference between getting it wrong and getting it right, is at least £175,000 per person.

Paul Stoltz and his team asked similar questions to 10,000 employers in the United States. Stoltz wanted to find out what personal attributes they prize most highly. He asked them who they would prefer to recruit and gave them two choices. The first was a person with the perfect skill set and qualifications. The second was a person with the right mindset.

WHAT'S THE COST OF GETTING IT WRONG?	WHAT'S THE UPSIDE WHEN YOU GET IT RIGHT?

Incredibly, 98 percent of the 10,000 employers surveyed chose option two: the person with the right mindset. The employers described 'the right mindset' by using words such as 'resilience' and 'grit'. Interestingly, Stoltz and his team then asked the employers how many 'normal' employees they would trade for just one who had the desired mindset. Incredibly, the answer was 7.3 on average. They would swap seven of their people for just one who had 'the right stuff'. When asked how many 'normal leaders' they would trade for a leader with the right mindset, this figure rose to an average of 8.4 (Stoltz, 2015).

Wow!!

Employers would trade eight of the leaders that they had hired, promoted, and retained, for just one who has the character they desire.

Culture is collective character.

In his book, *Making Character First*, Tom Hill (2010) shares his experiences of leading a manufacturing company in Oklahoma. Hill took the reins from his father-in-law who'd grown the business from scratch 30 years previously. Being based in a small town, the company started by employing people that the leaders knew personally. One of the benefits of a small town is that everyone knows everyone. If you were a pain-in-the-butt at school, everyone would know. So, in the early days, the business was able to recruit really good people and built a fantastic culture.

Over time though, it became a victim of its own success. The business grew rapidly and needed to recruit more people. Gradually the dynamics shifted. They became less picky as they became more desperate for people to fill roles. Instead of hiring really good people that they knew, they began to recruit anyone who could fill a role.

"Can you breathe?... Yes?... Great!... When can you start?"

Of course, this had a profound impact on the culture of the company. Adding the wrong kind of people diluted their once great culture.

Tom Hill noticed that the character of their people had a dramatic effect on almost every area of the business, so he instigated a change. They began focusing on their recruitment and developing their people. When they focused on recruiting and selecting those with 'the right character', and developing desirable characteristics in their people, their performance transformed. People became more motivated, productive, and creative. Their rates of absenteeism, health and safety incidents and disciplinary issues plummeted. The enormous rule book they had created became almost redundant. Managers spent more time solving operational challenges, such as how to improve working practices, and less on 'people issues'. As Tom Hill emphasises, a business is founded on people. Those with solid character tend to make good decisions because they want to do the right thing. Of course, the by-product is that strong performance and results then follow.

When I studied world-class individual performers, to find out what differentiated the very best in the world from the rest, I found the difference was character (Hartley, 2012). It wasn't their experience, knowledge, or skills... it was their character.

Over the years I've learned that truly world-class organisations recruit on character. They make sure they hire people who have the characteristics they require. Paul Stoltz found that many employers prize characteristics such as resilience. Others may seek people who have empathy, honesty, or tenacity. Whilst the specific characteristics may vary, there is a common core.

They are all recruiting on character!

I describe character as the outward expression of who I am. It's the way I live my personal values, beliefs, and philosophy. Importantly, it's more than just having the values. I could say that I value honesty. But, if I'm not truthful, I'm not demonstrating that value. To be an honest person, I need to live by that value, particularly when it would be easier not to.

This shows us that character operates on a deeper level than personality. Psychology defines personality as being the mental qualities that make us distinctive as individuals. Character has another dimension. Our character also includes our moral qualities.

Let's take a step back.

Why did I ask about the cost of getting it wrong and the value of getting it right?

Because hiring great people... hiring on character... is not easy.

It takes more time, demands more effort, and requires more thinking (although it doesn't usually cost much more money).

It is harder work.

So, it has to be worth it.

When we understand the cost of getting it wrong and the value of getting it right, we also realise why it's worth investing a little more time, energy and thinking to get great people.

CHAPTER ONE

How do you identify GREAT people?

I'll often ask sports coaches and business leaders a few questions.

"How do you identify talent and potential?"

"How do you know which of these people is made of 'the right stuff'?"

"What are the clues and signs?"

When it comes to hiring new people, most organisations rely on the usual suspect tools – CVs, interviews, references and maybe psychometrics. These tools are considered standard practice across business, education, healthcare, and many other walks of life.

But I have another question.

What do we learn about the person, using these tools?

What do we learn about their character from their CV... or during the interview... or from the results of a psychometric test?

When we stop and think about it, the answer tends to be, "Very little."

Their CV might tell us about their employment history. It could tell us which positions they've held, which job titles they've had, which organisations they've worked for and how long they stayed in the role... but it probably won't tell us how capable they were. The CV will also probably contain their educational history and relevant qualifications. If they wrote the CV themselves, which is not guaranteed, we might also see some language and presentational skills.

When I ask employers and hiring managers what they ultimately learn from a CV, the overriding answer is, "We learn what the candidate wants to tell us."

What about the interview then? What do we learn about a person's character through the interview?

When I've discussed this question with leaders, they tend to conclude that the value of an interview depends on the interviewer, the questions they ask, and how good they are at interpreting the answers. I've heard a lot of leaders talk about 'competency-based interviews', where they'll pose a scenario and ask what the candidate might do in that situation. I understand the rationale for these kinds of questions, but I also recognise that there are potential flaws in the process. These kinds of interviews will show whether a person knows what to do.

It doesn't tell us whether they will do it.

> There's often a sizeable gap between knowing what to do and actually doing it.

I remember being interviewed for my first ever job in Premier League football. I met the manager in a hotel. I was in my mid-twenties and although I'd been working in elite sport for around five years, I'd never worked with Premier League or international footballers. As part of the interview, he asked me, "What would you do if the players start playing up or messing about during a session?" Straight away I answered, "I'd put a rocket up their backside."

I knew it was the right answer. But, as I said it, I thought to myself... "Would I do that? I hope so."

In an interview, we could ask our candidate to tell us about a time when they've encountered a specific challenge. What we'll get in return is a story. It might be real. It might not be. It might be accurate. It might be exaggerated – human memory is fallible. It might be their story. It might be someone else's. The problem is... we don't really know.

Therefore, we may not actually learn very much about a person, or their character, from the conversation.

Interestingly, much of what we learn through the interview process often has little or no relation to the content of the interview itself. Many leaders talk about the impression a candidate makes. Did they arrive on time? Were they appropriately dressed? What preparation have they done? This information might actually tell us more about the person than their answers.

I've often asked employers and hiring managers where they think their recruitment process falls down. Interestingly, many of them reflect that they put too much emphasis on the rapport that is built during the interview. They'll say things like, "We seemed to get on really well" or "They seemed nice." And, whilst the ability to develop rapport is great, it might not be the overriding quality that you need in a candidate. Experience tells me that rapport does not necessarily lead to 'cultural fit'. A person might be easy to talk to (i.e., they can develop rapport), but do they embody your values (which is probably the true measure of cultural fit)?

> So perhaps we shouldn't allow rapport to have undue influence on our recruitment decisions.

―――――――――

What about psychometrics?

What do they tell us about a person?

Over the last 25 years of working in sport psychology I've used a wide range of psychometrics. I've learned that they can be very useful. Many people who use personality profiling tools are often astounded by how accurately the report describes them. Used properly, they can help us understand a person's tendencies.

Are they a detail-oriented person who will dot all the i's and cross all the t's?

Are they organised and methodical?

Are they action-oriented and goal-driven?

Are they a creative, lateral thinker?

Are they extrovert or introvert?

Are they people-oriented?

Whilst tools like this can be helpful, they also have their flaws. Most (if not all) are based on self-report or self-assessment. And although many have in-built validation and reliability mechanisms, it's possible to make them say what we want them to say. Honestly, I'm rubbish with detail! But, if I wanted my personality profile to say I was a great 'i-dotter and t-crosser', I could. So even psychometric tests are not infallible.

The other important realisation is that a personality profile helps us understand personality, not character. It might tell us whether they are an introvert or extrovert. But it doesn't tell us whether they're courageous... resilient... or honest.

Using CVs, interviews and psychometrics can give us some information. But how much do we learn about character?

———————

In my experience, world-class teams and organisations do use CVs, interviews, and psychometrics.

However, they don't rely on them!

They know that these tools won't give them the vital information they need about a person's character. So, if they want to be really confident in their hiring decisions, they need something else.

CHAPTER TWO

—

An important distinction
– Character ≠ Personality!

I'm going to interrupt this broadcast to draw a really important distinction.

Character is not the same as personality!

The dictionary defines personality as the mental qualities that make us distinctive as an individual. Character has another dimension. Our character also includes the moral qualities.

I've had a lot of conversations with leaders over the years who say, "We're looking to increase our diversity. Should we really be looking for people with common characteristics?"

It's a fair question. I understand the power of diversity. I actively encourage leaders to embrace diversity on many levels. At a fundamental level, this means we need to build teams of people who think differently, perceive things differently and have different ways of solving problems. All of this requires us to have a variety of personality types – linear thinkers, lateral thinkers, analytical people, creative people, etc.

However, it's also important that we share a set of common values and live by those. If we say we value honesty, we need honest people. If we value curiosity, we need curious people. Remember, our culture is collective character. If we don't get the character right, we're never going to get the culture right.

A client of mine was in the process of scaling his business. When we first chatted, they had 31 employees and were looking to recruit an additional 100 people within the next few years. Understandably, he was concerned that he might dilute their culture.

He described it by saying, "I've got two favourite flavours of ice cream – rum and raisin and honeycomb. At the moment, all 31 people are one of those two flavours. I really like all our people. What happens if I recruit a load of people I don't like?"

Using ice cream as an analogy, I said that having diverse personalities was like having different flavours. Honestly, his team will benefit from adding some mint choc chip, pistachio, and strawberry. However, he shouldn't compromise on quality.

The quality of the ice cream is like character. What he doesn't want is low quality, mass-produced, flavourless, budget ice cream. He wants premium quality, handmade ice cream, created with great ingredients by people who care. High quality ice cream in a range of different flavours is probably the optimal combination. It means that we get a diverse mix of different personalities who all share some critical characteristics.

03

CHAPTER THREE

—

Some Olympic thinking.

In 2006 I was thrown a challenge. I was working for an organisation called the English Institute of Sport. Our job was to provide sport science support to the Team GB Olympic programmes and England teams.

My challenge in 2006 was to help the GB Olympic programmes identify those athletes who had the potential to stand on the podium six years later, at the London 2012 Olympic Games. It was a pretty daunting task to be honest. When athletes stand on the podium, they're often in their late teens or early twenties (particularly in sports like swimming and gymnastics). Therefore, we needed to start identifying those who might have potential when they were 14, 15 and 16 years old.

I can remember standing on the side of a swimming pool one day watching dozens of swimmers ploughing up and down the pool. I asked myself, "How on earth do you identify a potential Olympic medal winner?"

As I chatted with the coaches, I realised that there is one thing that won't help – the stopwatch. The stopwatch is not a good indicator of potential. Looking at the results table doesn't help you identify potential. Those measures only tell you how fast a swimmer is today. And, with a teenage population, their speed today is often a result of maturation. If you take two 14-year-olds, one of them might be 6' 4" and the other is 4' 6". There's a good chance the 6' 4" swimmer will win today. But what happens when the smaller kid goes through their growth spurt? Who will win then?

So, I asked the coaches to tell me about the athletes they'd worked with in the past. Which of them went on to become champions? What were those athletes like when they were 14 years old?

Their answers were not that surprising to be honest.

"They had a really professional approach."

"They worked hard."

"They were hungry for feedback."

"They took responsibility for their performances."

"They drove their own improvement. They could assess their own performance. They were always looking at how they could get better."

"They could ride the bumps – injuries, loss of form, disappointments, etc."

Armed with this information, I started having a few focused conversations with the swimmers as they came into training. As a young lad walked through the door early one morning, I remember asking him, "What are you working on today?"

"I dunno", he grunted.

"Okay", I replied… and off he went.

I then asked a second swimmer, "What are you working on today?"

"I need to work on my turns", he replied.

"Ah, interesting", I said, "Why turns?"

"I've had a few competitions during the last few weeks, and I've noticed my turns are a bit ropey. Some are okay, but some are a bit rubbish. The other day I came into the wall in first place and went out in fifth… so I need to work on my turn", he said.

As I watched these two swimmers during their session, I noticed the first one going through the motions. He'd swim up and down with everyone else, but without a great deal of purpose. When the coach told them all to go flat-out, he cruised in for the last few metres. When the coach was giving the group feedback, he was chatting to his mate.

The second swimmer, on the other hand, was focused. Although not all his turns were perfect, I could see him working on them. Occasionally, he'd ask one of the coaches for feedback.

At the end of the session, I parked myself next to the door again. When the first lad walked past, munching on a chocolate bar, I asked, "How was the session?"

"Alright", he grunted.

As the second one wandered past, I asked the same question.

"Yeah, they're better", he replied, "I've realised that my approach into the wall is really important. If I take my last stroke too late, I get too crunched up, so I can't get my feet over the top... then I can't plant them on the wall properly... so I don't get a powerful push off. And, if I glide into the wall, I lose all my speed."

The following morning, I go through the same routine – "What are you working on today?" The first lad grunts back and shrugs again. The second lad looks at me like I'm a bit thick.

"Still turns", he replies.

Just for interest, which one of these two athletes do you think has a better chance of standing on the podium in six years' time?

If you look at their results, you may not see much difference over the course of a week or even a month. However, in a few months you'll probably notice a gap starting to appear. After six months I saw the second lad qualifying for national competitions. He was also selected for a national training squad. Interestingly, when that happened, the first lad struggled to figure out why he hadn't been chosen. When he saw his teammate selected ahead of him, he said, "I don't get it. We've been doing exactly the same training."

There are a few similar examples from the NFL too. In 1956 the Green Bay Packers drafted a quarterback called Bart Starr. He was the stellar player of his generation. Bart Starr played at the Packers for 16 seasons, winning three consecutive Superbowl titles – a feat which has never been equalled. He was named the Superbowl MVP (Most Valuable Player) twice and became the League MVP.

Amazingly, Bart Starr was drafted in the 17th round, as the 200th overall pick. He was the third-choice quarterback at the University of Alabama. So, why did the Packers draft him? And how did he go on to become a superstar player?

Interestingly, Jack Vainisi, the Packers Personnel Director, knew the basketball coach at the University of Alabama – a man called Johnny Dee. Johnny Dee noticed that Bart Starr was a great learner. He was always in the gym, working hard on his game, seeking input from his coaches, and learning quickly. It was these qualities that persuaded the Packers to sign him. These were the signs that Bart Starr had the potential to become a truly great player (Devaney, 1967).

I know these are both examples from sport.

But how does this thinking apply to you?

How could you use it to help you recruit great people?

HOW DOES THIS THINKING APPLY TO YOU?
HOW COULD YOU USE IT TO HELP YOU RECRUIT GREAT PEOPLE?

CHAPTER FOUR

What characteristics do you need?

My brain only operates on one level – simple. Hiring great people is pretty simple. Of course, simple doesn't mean easy. But it's not a complicated process at all – just a handful of critical steps.

The first step is to identify the characteristics you need in your people.

When many people embark on this process, they fall into a trap. The trap is to describe a superhuman. They write down every positive characteristic they can think of.

"We need someone who is honest, has integrity, is resilient, has empathy, is a self-starter, is brilliant with detail, is strategic and creative, can see the bigger picture, etc. etc. etc." You get the idea, I'm sure. The obvious problem is that we're highly unlikely to find a superhuman.

The other trap people often fall into is describing the polar opposite of the person who just failed in the role. Understanding what doesn't work can provide us with insights. However, it doesn't necessarily mean that we need someone who is the polar opposite. The person who didn't work might have had some of the characteristics we need, just not all of them. They might have had a couple of truly great qualities, but these were overshadowed by one undesirable characteristic.

So, it's often wise to step back and start our thinking with a clean slate.

I've come to realise that the characteristics we need fall into a couple of categories.

Organisational characteristics

There are characteristics that we want everyone in the organisation to have. Culture is collective character. It is the culmination of the characteristics our people display. If we want honesty to be a feature of our culture, it makes sense to recruit honest people.

Role characteristics

Sometimes there are specific characteristics that we need for a particular role. For example, this role may need someone who has more tenacity, resilience, or composure. Other roles might require patience or empathy. When we understand the characteristics needed for a particular role, we can look for people who have them.

———————

Once upon a time a client asked me to help them recruit for a brand-new position. They were a fast-growing engineering business who designed, made, and sold gas analysers. Up to that point, the repairs' function had been picked up by one of the spare engineers. But, as the company grew, they needed a specialist repairs person.

I remember chatting to Paul, who was recruiting for the position. I asked him what characteristics they needed in this person. We explored the question, throwing all sorts of possibilities around. After a while he said, "I need someone that will just keep going at a problem... someone who might go down a dead end, but then come back, try again, look for a new avenue... and keep going until they solve it. I need a detective. I need Sherlock!"

———————

I'm a great believer that clarity is extremely powerful. When we know what we're looking for, we stand a much better chance of finding it.

Over the years, I've asked similar questions to other organisations that want to hire great people. The majority can't describe it through one persona (e.g., Sherlock). Instead, they have a range of characteristics that they need.

Who do you need?

Start by thinking about your very best people.

What were they like?

Who has surprised you?

Who did you think might not make the grade, but went on to become a superstar?

Have you recruited people you thought would be amazing, but who didn't deliver?

What were they like?

Sometimes, the answers surprise us. I asked a Sales Manager to reflect on the characteristics he saw in his highest performers. He had a telesales team. Over the years, he'd focused on hiring people who were chatty and could develop rapport quickly. They tended to be more extrovert than introvert. However, when he stepped back, he noticed that his best performers were organised and methodical. They were also great at managing their pipeline and following up with people. Often, they were the quieter and more reserved members of the team, not the loud and outgoing ones. They were also more curious and tended to listen rather than talk.

What kind of characteristics do you see in your very best performers?

As you throw ideas around, you might generate a dozen or so potential characteristics. This gives us a good place to start. Once you have a decent list, it's time to refine it down to three or four critical characteristics. I do have a client who has five, but I wouldn't recommend any more than that. Importantly, these are the most important three or four characteristics.

In fact, I'll go one step further. I'll challenge you to put these characteristics in rank order.

If you could only have one, which would you choose? Which one is the most important?

Then, if you could add a second, which one would you include?

What about a third?

Working on this basis forces us to be ruthless and scrutinise our thinking.

Which characteristics really are critical?

Which ones would we sacrifice?

Which ones are non-negotiables?

What qualities will enable people to be successful in this organisation, and in this role?

———————

Here are a few examples from my clients.

A technology supplier (that sells hardware, software, cloud solutions, cyber security, etc.) was recruiting sales executives that would work from home. They needed people who were...
Resilient
Organised
Coachable
Self-starters

A construction company that builds retirement housing were also recruiting sales executives. They needed people who had...
Tenacity
Empathy
Adaptability

A recruitment agency, which specialises in helping their clients find senior finance professionals, are always on the lookout for great consultants. They describe their ideal candidates using the acronym T.R.I.C.O.
Teamwork
Resilience
Initiative
Consultative nature
Own your own improvement.

———————

Experience tells me that it's relatively easy to come up with the words. However, we also need to know what we mean by them. If we're part of an organisation, we need to share this, so that everyone understands what's meant by a word like 'resilience' and how we recognise someone who is resilient. If we say we're looking for honesty, what does that mean? Are we saying we will only employ people that have never told a lie in their entire life? Or do we mean something else?

A few years ago, I was thinking about taking on a digital marketing apprentice for our business. So, I stepped back and thought about the characteristics we needed. How would I know if the person in front of me was a potential superstar?

I narrowed it down to the following four characteristics. Here's how I communicated them through the job description.

I'm looking for someone who is...

- Curious... someone who is 'a sponge' and is hungry to learn.

- Caring... someone who doesn't just want to do the job... they want to do it REALLY well!

- Enterprising... someone who can solve problems, figure things out, come up with ideas and put them into action.

- Honest... someone who is truthful, fair, respectful... someone who can give honest feedback and have open, honest conversations.

———————

Of course, once you've refined your list, it's wise to validate it.

Are these the characteristics that you see in your very best people?

How do they demonstrate these characteristics through their choices, decisions, and actions?

Once you have identified the key characteristics, you're ready for the next step.

CHAPTER FIVE

——

How do you know which candidates have these characteristics?

There's a simple way to discover whether the candidates in front of you possess the characteristics you need.

Test them.

Provide a challenge that makes your candidates demonstrate these characteristics!

Then... observe their response.

——

Importantly, 'test them' does not mean 'ask them'. To test people, we need to put them in a challenging situation and see how they respond. Of course, the challenges we create need to test the characteristics we're looking for.

For example, imagine you needed your people to be courageous. Courage is the ability to step towards the things we're scared of. So, to test courage, we'd need to put people face to face with one of their fears and then see how they respond. If we knew that the candidate was scared of spiders, we could bring in a tarantula, pop it on the desk and see how they respond. Do they run screaming for the hills? Or do they hold their ground, despite being scared? Would they go a stage further and step towards it? If a person wasn't scared of spiders, this situation won't test their courage. To see courage, we would need to know what they feared.

There are some usual suspects that tend to make most people's heart race... like speaking in public, singing in public, or being put in the spotlight. People tend to fear failure, so putting them in a position where they could fail might also provide a test of courage.

These are a couple of examples of how we could test just one characteristic – courage. To find out whether your candidates have the characteristics you need, you'll need to present challenges that test those qualities. Importantly, the test we provide needs to be contextually close to the challenges they'll encounter in the role.

Here are a few examples that are perfectly designed for the organisations that employ them, and the context in which they operate.

The Special Air Service (SAS) is an elite regiment of the British Army. SAS units are often tasked to take on the toughest missions in the most extreme conditions. The SAS knows that these missions will push their soldiers to the limit. Therefore, to be successful, recruits need to have some critical characteristics, such as tenacity.

I describe tenacity as the ability to keep going, no matter what. In the SAS, that means being able to push yourself well beyond the pain barrier. If a soldier quits because the mission is too tough or too much, they could be captured (and probably tortured) or killed.

So, how do they find out how tenacious their candidates are?

They could ask them. They could invite candidates to tell them a time when they faced an extreme challenge and how they got through. But that's not going to demonstrate whether they have what it takes. So, they set them a challenge. They put a 30kg pack on their backs and tell them to walk (Hayes, 2021). If you were given this challenge, I suspect one of your first questions would be, "How far?" The answer is... "Until we tell you to stop." That's a pretty daunting prospect. Are they saying walk for a few hours, or days, or a week, or a month? Very simply, they need to walk until they're told to stop.

What happens if they get blisters?

They keep walking.

What happens if they break both legs?

They crawl.

Importantly, their decisions and actions demonstrate whether they have the tenacity. The officers who are recruiting the next intake of soldiers don't need to guess whether these candidates are tenacious. The test tells them.

The US Navy SEALs famously use a similar test. They bury their candidates up to their necks in freezing cold sand. It's incredibly uncomfortable. Coupled with the extreme discomfort, the candidates are also told they can quit at any time. All they have to do is say they've had enough, and they will be pulled out of the sand and provided with a nice warm bath. Of course, it'll also be the end of their journey in the SEALs (Willink and Babin, 2015).

Obviously, these tests are specifically designed for their context. They have been created to test an element of tenacity that is critical in these particular roles. It's not appropriate for everyone, but it's ideal for elite special forces soldiers.

Here's another example from an elite team.

The Red Arrows are the Royal Air Force (RAF) aerobatic display team. Their display routines are incredible and push the team of nine pilots to their limits. Interestingly, every year the most senior three members are 'retired' (which often means moving to other jobs within the RAF). Therefore, each year, the team need to recruit three new pilots to the team. It's a job that many pilots dream of so, historically, they tend to have 30-40 applicants for three slots.

How do they decide which of these 30-40 applicants has what it takes to become 'a Red'?

I posed this question to Jas Hawker, a former Red Arrows team leader. He started by saying that they're not looking for the three best pilots.

"What????", I replied, "I've seen what you guys do. It's crazy! You fly in close formation, at hundreds of miles an hour, doing loop-the-loops and high-speed passes, with just a couple of feet between your wing tips. What do you mean you don't recruit the best three pilots?"

"No", he said, "They do have to be good enough as a pilot. We do have a flying skills test, which they need to pass. But, once we know their flying is good enough, we're not looking at their skills. We're looking for the three best team players."

Wow.

When I think about it, this makes complete sense. Over the years I've asked dozens of world-class leaders how they create truly great teams. Most of them will tell you that having great team players is a fundamental ingredient (Hartley, 2015).

So, how do they identify great team players?

Jas Hawker told me that they whittle down their 30-40 applicants to a shortlist of nine, who join them for a week's training camp. Whilst they're away for the week, the candidates are put in challenging positions and the team observe their responses. For example, they know that all nine of the prospective pilots will be pushed right to the edge of their abilities. Therefore, they'll all make mistakes.

The question is... how do they respond?

Are they willing to put their hands up and take responsibility?

Are they willing to take critical feedback?

Do they use this feedback to improve?

Are they willing to ask for help?

What are they like 'under pressure'?

The team also know that during the regular course of daily life in the team, there are a lot of jobs that need doing... including the very mundane, unsexy, 'dirty' jobs. Do the candidates roll up their sleeves and get on with them? Or are they only interested in the high octane, exciting, sexy parts of the job?

Do they put their own interests before the team's, or the team's interests first?

During the week's training camp, the team will 'get their eye in'. They will look for the clues and signs that tell them which candidates are the best team players. By observing people's responses to the challenges, they build up a bank of evidence. It is this evidence that informs their recruitment decisions.

Several years ago, I was approached by a friend who worked for an NBA franchise in the US. He asked me to help devise a way to assess 'grit' in basketball players. Every year they drafted players from colleges. They had a variety of physical tests, medical tests, skills tests and even psychometrics. But experience told them, when it came to mental toughness, they occasionally got it right but often got it wrong.

To help them assess mental toughness, we selected a set of simple challenges. All the tests were based on activities and exercises they already used. For example, they would test the players' skills (e.g., shooting accuracy) and physical fitness (strength, speed, endurance, etc.). As with all good tests, there is normally a point at which the players will fail (e.g., a weight they can no longer lift, or a jump they can't make or a shot they miss). The question is, how do they respond when they get to that point?

Do they get defensive?

Do they look to blame something?

Do they become demoralised?

What happens if their failure is public?

What happens if they get criticised?

Of course, all these challenges come as part of the package for players in the NBA. All players have good days and bad days. Their performances will be constantly under the scrutiny of coaches, teammates, the media, social media, the fans, etc.

How resilient are they?

How do they bounce back from setbacks?

Whilst the NBA franchise had the tests in place, they didn't know how to observe and assess the response. So, I created *The Mental Toughness Matrix* (Fig. 1). This gave them a common frame of reference. It helped everyone understand what we were looking for and what 'mental toughness' meant – literally what it looked like and sounded like when players demonstrated it. And it gave everyone involved in the process – basketball coaches, physiotherapists, strength and conditioning coaches, performance analysts, etc. – a way to assess the response they observed and 'measure' it using the same scale.

TRAIT	NOT SO TOUGH	
Consistency in Adverse Conditions	Can be significantly affected by relatively small adverse events. Performance often declines after situational changes.	Performance can be affected by relatively minor adverse conditions, but the fluctuation is less significant.
Response to Set-Backs	Tends to experience significant knocks when they encounter set-backs. Normally emerges weaker as a result. Set-backs can be catastrophic.	Set-backs tend to leave 'scars'. Normally, the person does not return from the event as strongly. They tend to view set-backs as negative.
Composure Under Pressure	Often perceives 'pressure' in a situation and tends to crumble - makes strange decisions, abandons the game plan, panics and makes significant errors.	Becomes erratic and prone to errors when situations turn against them or if they perceive they are 'under pressure'.
Appetite for Discomfort Zone	Actively avoids their discomfort zone and consciously backs away from challenges that push them.	Will occasionally enter their discomfort zone for short periods if the situation demands.
Willingness to Push to The Linit	Tends to give up before things become uncomfortable. (Has no idea where their true limit is.)	Normally gives up at the point of mild discomfort or early experiences of discomfort.
Perception of Critical Feedback	Struggles to accept criticism and tends to ignore it.	Will accept some critical feedback, often begrudgingly, and occasionally acts upon it.

		TOUGH
Resistant to the more minor adverse conditions but can be affected by more difficult situations.	Performance is generally stable but can be affected by extreme adversity. However, performance swings are likely to be smaller.	Maintains focus, consistently delivers the processes with high quality execution in any situation.
Tends not to be knocked by set-backs and normally comes back to a point of parity from any event.	Can gain from and learn from set-backs, finding opportunities that can give them some advantage.	Uses set-backs as an opportunity to strengthen. As a result they consistently emerge stronger from an event.
Can become erratic or prone to errors that they perceive to be 'highly pressurised'.	May become either slightly more conservative or take more risks in situations they perceive as 'highly pressurised'.	Consistent in their decision-making, adherence to the game plan, focus and execution, in any situation.
Will push into their discomfort zone when the need demands but will normally only remain there as long as the demand remains.	Will choose to operate on the edge of their comfort/discomfort zone regularly and take more significant strides into discomfort occasionally.	Actively seeks opportunities to take significant steps into their discomfort zone.
Will endure discomfort on a needs-must basis but tends not to endure significant discomfort for extended periods.	Will ensure signficant discomfort for extended periods and operate close to their true limits.	Will push it until breaking point so that they know their true limit, and then operate very close to the limit regularly.
Accepts critical feedback comfortably and often uses it.	Readily accepts and uses critical feedback regularly, and views it as an opportunity to improve.	Actively seeks critical feedback, is proactively self-critical and works to get the maximum benefit from it.

Fig. 1 – The Mental Toughness Matrix (Hartley, 2018).

I know that these examples come from world-class organisations. Realistically, you may not be able to take candidates away to a training camp in Cyprus for a week, like the Red Arrows do (although it's worth considering ☺).

So, here's another example of how to test. Do you remember me mentioning a set of characteristics I identified for a digital marketing apprentice: curious, caring, enterprising and honest?

The tests I devised are shown on page 48.

As a digital marketing apprentice, they need to be capable of understanding an audience, reaching that audience and creating messages that engage them. So, our candidates' first challenge was to understand me. I was their audience. To get them started, we gave them a little information about me – just the basic profile, such as age, gender, occupation, and some interests. We also pointed them in the direction of my social media profiles. The information we provided was deliberately brief. I wanted to know whether they were curious to find out more. Would they actively learn more about me, so that they could really engage me (their audience) and get my attention?

How curious were they? Would they follow their curiosity?

The first part of the challenge was crucial, because it would give them a foundation for the next part. Once they'd found out about their audience, we challenged them to create a campaign and sell something. In this case, the job was to sell themselves. They needed to create a campaign that showed me who they are and why they'd be great for this role. Importantly, we didn't provide any boundaries for this. They were free to use whatever formats (video, images / memes, blogs, podcasts, etc.) and platforms (Facebook, Twitter, TikTok, Instagram, etc.) they wanted. Obviously, it would be wise to use platforms that their audience (i.e., me) uses and formats their audience typically engages with. By leaving it completely open, I can start to see how enterprising and entrepreneurial they are.

Can they operate without instructions?

How innovative are they?

Can they formulate a strategy on their own?

Can they execute it?

We also asked them to 'show their workings'.

Why did they adopt this strategy? What options did they consider? Which did they reject? What was their thought process?

When we look at the campaign they created, we can see the quality of their work and their attention to detail. How much time and effort did they put into it? How much do they care about their work? How much do they care about getting this job?

So far, our process helps us to assess how curious, enterprising, and caring our candidates are. If you remember, we're also looking for people who are honest. In particular, we want to know that they will honestly reflect on their own performance and engage in open, honest conversations.

Therefore, during the interview we provided two more challenges. The first was to assess their own campaign. What worked well? What have they learned? What would they do differently next time? This can be quite tough for some people. How honest are they willing to be when assessing their own performance?

However, the second challenge is probably tougher. We asked them to critique one of our own social media campaigns – our 'Advent calendar' (24 memes, posts, and YouTube clips that we shared with our followers during December). We're not social media or digital marketing experts. So, we know there will be loads we can improve on. I want to know how we can make it better. More importantly, I want to know who is willing to be honest with us.

Who will tell us what they really think and deliver their feedback in a respectful way, which helps us to improve?

How our candidates respond to these challenges will show us how curious, caring, enterprising and honest they are.

―――――――

I do know that creating these tests can be a challenge in itself. Having been through the process with dozens of organisations, there are a few approaches that I've found helpful.

―――――――

Characteristics to Identify

1. **LEARNER / CURIOUS**
2. **ENTERPRISING / ENTREPRENEURIAL**
3. **HONEST / SELF-REFLECTIVE**
4. **CARES** (about doing a great job)

The Test we Devised

1 LEARNER / CURIOUS

Give instructions
- How to impress Simon

→

2 ENTERPRISING / ENTREPRENEURIAL

Create a campaign that tells us who you are and why you'd be great at this job.

No set format - could be webpage, video, Insta post blog...?

3 HONEST / SELF-REFLECTIVE

Here's our 'Advent Calendar' campaign. What do you think?

↑

3 HONEST / SELF-REFLECTIVE

How would you self-assess your application campaign?
What have you learned?
What would you do next time?

←

4 CARES (about doing a great job)

Show your workings
Why did you decide to do it this way?
What's your quality / attention to detail like?
How much effort / application did you invest?

Employ some '11 star thinking'

'11 star thinking' is based on the principle that Airbnb founder, Brian Chesky, shared with Reid Hoffmann during an episode of the Masters of Scale podcast. It describes how Airbnb stretched their people to think beyond the norm. They wanted to create amazing experiences that their guests would rave about. This meant going way beyond the '5 star' experience their customers would get from a top hotel. To do it, they encouraged their people to imagine an '11 star' experience and then work backwards until we reach something that is feasible (Gallagher, 2017).

I used a similar approach when helping a client to hire for a senior position in his business. He was looking for someone to head up his HR Recruitment Team. When I asked what characteristics he required, my client said, "I need someone who is entrepreneurial... who is driven... committed... and will do whatever it takes to be successful." Now, we could legitimately debate whether these are the most critical characteristics or not. However, if those are the most important qualities, we need to find a way to test for them.

So, I asked, "What would happen if we told your candidates that the interview was at 7am, on a Sunday morning, in one of those little stone huts (known as a bothy) in the middle of the Cairngorms (the mountain range in the Highlands of Scotland)?"

He thought about it for moment and then replied, "Well, just to get there, they'd have to... get up ridiculously early, drive to Scotland, figure out how to navigate to the bothy, plan their route, get all the protective gear, trek through the mountains...." He paused for a moment. "Just to get there, they'd have to show all the qualities I need", he said.

"So, what would you ask at interview when they arrived?", I asked.

"Tea or coffee?", he replied.

Now, I freely admit that this may not be practical or sensible. But it's an example of '11 star' thinking. Although we may not use that exact test, once we've stretched it, we can work backwards to find something that is feasible.

This is how they mapped out the experience when someone arrives at their Airbnb – from '1 star' to '11 star'. Interestingly, 'feasible' is often a higher standard than we might think.

Airbnb's 11-Star Framework

"You have to almost design the extreme to come backwards."
~ Brian Chesky

Refund me — 1
Knock on door
No response

I had to wait — 2
Knock on door
Waited 20 minutes for the host

Expected experience — 5
Knock on door
The host opens and lets you in

THE LINES OF FEASIBILITY

Love it more than a hotel — 6
Knock on door
Host welcomes and shows you around
Apartment is stocked with water and toiletries

Way beyond — 7
Knock on door
Host personalises your experience
"I know you like surfing. Here's a surfboard.
Here's my car. Also here's a suprise booking for
the best restaurant in town."

Beatles check-in — 10
Get off plane
Welcomed by 5,000 high-school kids cheering
your name
Car pick-up ready
Arrive at Airbnb and a press conference is
waiting for you

Elon Musk — 11
Show up at the airport and Elon Musk is there.
Elon Musk just says "you're going to space."

Use real-life challenges that test your people.

Do you remember the engineering company who were looking for Sherlock?

Once we knew that they needed a detective, we could set about finding one. After a little discussion, Paul and I agreed on a test. He selected their trickiest repair job to date. Paul knew that finding the cause and repairing the fault would probably take a decent engineer about six hours. For the purposes of a recruitment challenge, they gave their candidates an hour.

The aim was not to see if anyone could achieve the impossible. The aim was to see how they responded to the challenge and how they approached it. The company had shortlisted five candidates. The first one looked at the challenge and said, "That's impossible. There's no point even starting." He folded his arms and refused to start. Three of the candidates started, hit a couple of dead ends, and gave up.

But one candidate just kept going. They tried a few things, hit dead ends, started again, looked at other avenues and worked their way through the challenge. After an hour Paul told the candidate, "Time's up." The candidate replied, "Don't stop me now, I've only just got going."

Interestingly, after looking at their CVs and interviewing the five they'd shortlisted, Paul said the candidates were evenly matched. However, after giving them the test, one stood out. Unsurprisingly, they offered him the job. After a few weeks I asked Paul what he thought of his new recruit. He replied, "Such a good fit – like a hand in a glove."

When this same company were looking to recruit a new member of their Research and Development (R&D) team, they gave their candidates 'the SpaceX challenge'. Simply put, they literally gave candidates the project brief that SpaceX had given the company and said, "What would you do with that?" The company knew that this particular project had really stretched their R&D team. It had also identified those members of the team who were the more innovative, enterprising, and creative. Therefore, they already knew that it would test these same characteristics in their candidates.

———————

A marketing agency valued people who were entrepreneurial – those who could identify problems, come up with solutions and put them into action. To help develop these characteristics, we created an 'away day' and gave their people a challenge.

In teams of eight, your mission is to raise as much money as possible for our chosen charity between 10am and 4pm.

You have a range of resources that the charity has provided – t-shirts, collection buckets, permission from the local council to fundraise in the city, etc.

You have a dedicated 'war room' with flip charts, pens, a couple of laptops, WiFi, etc.

Go!

As their team got to work, the leaders observed. Through the course of the day, they learned a huge amount about their people.

Who stepped up to lead?

Who were the great team players?

Who asked the challenging questions?

Who were the entrepreneurial thinkers?

This simple exercise helped identify and develop this entrepreneurial characteristic. So, when it came to recruiting new people, the business simply gave candidates a similar challenge – work as a team to raise as much money as possible for the charity in a fixed time frame with a set of resources.

Then, they stepped back and observed the response.

––––––––––––

Okay, those are a few real-life examples of how other people test for the characteristics they need.

Time to get your thinking apparatus engaged on this.

How could you start to test the characteristics you need in your people?

WHAT CHARACTERISTICS DO YOU NEED?	HOW COULD YOU TEST FOR THEM?
1	
2	
3	
4	

CHAPTER SIX

—

How can we make it practical?

When people start devising tests, they often think, "How are we supposed to do all this? It would take us days."

As we said at the very start of this book, recruiting on character often takes more time, effort, and energy. We need to be prepared for that.

But it also needs to be practical.

Many organisations struggle because they are trying to squeeze it all into a tiny portion of the recruitment timeline. Normally, they're trying to do everything within the interview or during an assessment day. Experience tells me that we often get far more value when we optimise the whole of the timeline. In my view, the timeline starts before we even send an advert and continues way beyond 'probation'. However, many organisations only use a very small section of this – normally from application (or shortlisting) to the point at which they make an offer.

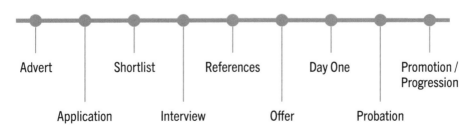

I mentioned a construction company that needed great sales executives. They identified three critical characteristics – tenacity, empathy, and adaptability. To see how adaptable and flexible candidates were, they said, "To apply for the role, don't just send us your CV. As well as your CV, send us a little selfie video (30-60 seconds) telling us a little bit about yourself and why you're interested in this job."

To be honest, they weren't looking for highly trained TV presenters that were wonderful in front of the camera. They were looking for people who were adaptable. They wanted people who were willing to try something outside of their comfort zone... able to just give it a go.

It was a great way to test adaptability at the point of application. They didn't need to wait until the interview or create an exercise for an assessment day. If people couldn't send a selfie video, they wouldn't even get shortlisted. So, it helped them filter out candidates who didn't have this characteristic very early in the process.

It also enabled them to explore another characteristic during the interview. They'd ask how many attempts the candidate had tried before they had a selfie video they were happy to send. Was it the first attempt... fifth... tenth... twentieth? How many times had they tried? Tenacity is our ability to keep going and not quit. So, this test also gave them a useful clue about tenacity.

Once the candidates had sent their CV plus the selfie video, the company gave them another challenge. Their team of sales executives were assigned specific sites. The job required them to create a strategy to sell all the properties on their sites. It required them to work some unsociable hours and to travel. So, the next challenge was to create a strategy for a particular site and present it during the interview. In order to create their strategy, candidates would have to do some research. Ideally, they'd need to visit one of the sites, have a look around, get a feel for it and then incorporate what they'd learned in their strategy. So, once an applicant had been shortlisted, the company gave them this challenge and details of where to find the sites.

Some candidates said, "I'm not travelling to a site. I haven't got time for that."

As far as the company was concerned, that is great information! If someone is not willing to travel or dedicate some time to this, they're never going to become successful in the role.

When we use the recruitment timeline well, we create hurdles for candidates to jump over. As well as testing the characteristics we're looking for, there is a secondary benefit. We also test their commitment.

So, before a candidate even came in for interview, the construction company has already learned about their tenacity and adaptability. But what about their empathy? How do they know whether a candidate listens to others, cares about their issues, and has a genuine desire to help? To test empathy, the company employed 'the receptionist test'.

When candidates arrived for interview, they met June (the receptionist). June was chatty. Whilst they were waiting to be called for interview, June would introduce herself. She'd tell them all about her son, who'd been in a motorbike accident recently. He'd broken his leg and was a bit bruised but, fortunately, was on the mend. Of course, it all meant that June had been back and forth to the hospital recently and was constantly worrying about her son.

Each of the candidates heard June's story. When they arrived in the interview room, they were asked if they'd met the receptionist.

Interviewer: "Good morning. Thanks for coming. Have you been offered a drink?"

Candidate: "Yes, thank you."

Interviewer: "Super. So, you met our receptionist?"

Candidate: "Oh yes."

Interviewer: "What's her name?"

Some candidates: "... Uh..."

Interviewer: "Did she tell you anything about herself?"

Quite a few candidates: ".... Uh..." (as they shift awkwardly in their seats).

———————

Overleaf is an example of the timeline that the construction company built. It gave them a great way of testing their three critical characteristics at various stages of the process.

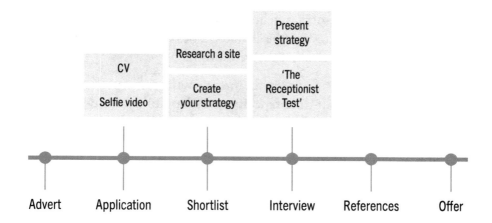

Advert Application Shortlist Interview References Offer

CHAPTER SEVEN

—

How to validate the tests.

Do the tests you've chosen give an accurate reflection of the characteristics you need?

If they do, it stands to reason that your best people will perform really well in the test, and your not-so-great people will struggle.

This simple understanding helps us to validate our tests.

The construction company that employed the selfie video test validated it with their own team. They asked their current sales executives to film a 30-60 second selfie video on their phone, introducing themselves and talking about why they enjoyed their role.

Interestingly, the Sales Director had classified her team into 'Ones', 'Twos' and 'Threes'.

'Ones' were her top performers.

'Twos' were her middle performers.

'Threes' were her bottom performers.

It probably won't surprise you to know that her 'Ones' created their selfie videos and sent them in. The higher performing 'Twos' did the same. However, the lower performing 'Twos' and 'Threes' found all kinds of excuses not to film and submit a selfie video.

So, to validate your tests, simply challenge your current people.

Do your better people perform better in the test?

If so, it's probably a good indicator. If not, it's probably wise to learn, adapt and try something else.

CHAPTER EIGHT

—

How to become a magnet for talent.

As I'm sure you'll have noticed, hiring on character is a process of attrition. We're deliberately placing hurdles in the path of our candidates – making the journey tougher for them. Of course, it means that not everyone will make it through the process. We'll lose people along the way.

Whilst many employers understand the importance of being picky, there's often some resistance.

"We have a vacancy to fill."

"We don't have many applicants."

"If our process is too long, or too demanding, the candidates will take the easier option and we'll end up with no-one."

These are very valid concerns. An organisation can't function without people. It's also true that many candidates will prefer the easier route. However, those people that choose the easiest path may not have the characteristics that you prize.

So, what's the solution?

———

I've noticed that world-class organisations can test their candidates, because they have a queue outside the door.

They have become a 'magnet for talent' as I describe it – a place that great people want to be.

As a kid, I wanted to be a pilot and fly fast jets. It was my dream to fly in the Red Arrows. I suspect I'm not alone. It's also an aspiration for many of the fast jet pilots within the Royal Air Force. No doubt that's why, historically, they have 30-40 applicants each year all vying for three spots on the team.

The SAS have created a similar demand. Despite a notoriously gruelling selection process, in which candidates have died, the SAS and SBS (Special Boat Service) still have an average of 125 candidates from which only 10 will be selected (Elite UK Forces, 2023).

Most (if not all) of the world-class organisations have become magnets for talent. Of course, it doesn't take a genius to figure out how this works. These organisations are the best. They're widely regarded as the best in their field. So, the very best people want to join them.

Having a queue of extremely good people outside the door, who all want to be part of the organisation, is a critical first step in the recruitment process. Most leaders that I've met will say...

"Yes, that all makes sense. However, we're not the Red Arrows or the SAS. We're not world famous. There isn't a queue outside our door."

So, how do you create the queue?

Once upon a time, I was the Chair of Governors at our daughters' primary school. At the beginning of my tenure, I had a conversation with our Head Teacher about recruitment. We had a bit of a revolving door. As the Head Teacher explained it, "We just can't get good teachers." She went on to describe the last two recruitment drives. We placed a standard advertisement on the Local Authority job board and had a handful of applicants, none of whom really impressed. Our Head Teacher and the recruitment committee then shortlisted a couple for interview and ended up offering the job to one of them. Her words were, "We can't have a class of children with no teacher, so we end up taking the best of a bad bunch." She also explained that, as a small rural village primary school with less than 100 children, we weren't the kind of place that an ambitious young teacher would tend to choose.

When I was at school we studied magnetism in science, and I noticed a few things. A magnet has a pole that attracts and a pole that repels. I also noticed that magnets don't attract every material. They do attract some metals, but they don't attract wood or plastic.

So, to become magnetic, we need to ask a few questions.

Who do we want to attract?

What would attract that kind of person?

Why would our ideal candidate want to work here, with us?

So, I asked a few very good teachers to describe the kind of school they'd love to work in. Interestingly they said...

"A friendly school ... with really nice children, who are polite and well behaved ... and a lovely staff team ... where everyone takes pride in what they do and how they do it."

So, for the next 12 to 18 months we focused our efforts on making sure that everyone who visited our school went away saying exactly these things. During the natural course of business, we'd be visited by Educational Advisors from the Local Authority, Bursars, trades people, other teachers and Head Teachers, parents, and so on. And, as you'd expect, people talk to each other. If you're a good school, word gets around.

We advertised a teaching post a couple of years later. We had eight applicants and shortlisted five for interview. Of the five, two were very strong candidates. We'd have been delighted with either, but only had one vacancy, so we offered the job to the best candidate.

When our Head Teacher announced her retirement, we did some more work to build on this. Incredibly, for a small village primary school, we had the joint highest number of applicants in the Local Authority's history. To put that into perspective, we had more applicants that the biggest secondary schools in the area. We had planned to shortlist the best four but ended up selecting five (because we had five extremely strong candidates). Following the interviews and assessment day, we had refined this to a final three, all of whom were more than capable of doing a great job. Obviously, there was only one vacancy, so we had to choose someone.

Importantly, we'd created a queue outside the door. We had become a school that our ideal candidates wanted to join.

The engineering business that recruited Sherlock had a similar challenge. They were a company of around 70 people, based in a small market town in North Yorkshire. They are miles away from cities like York and Leeds that are home to specialist manufacturing and engineering companies. One day the Managing Director asked me, "How can we attract great engineers to work here? We're almost an hour from York and Harrogate, and even further from Leeds."

I replied, "Good question! Why would the very best engineers want to work here?"

He paused for a moment and then said, "The North York Moors are beautiful. You can go cycling or walking in the hills."

"That's great", I said, "But how many engineers are bothered about cycling and walking in the hills?"

"Well, that's the problem", he replied, "Not many."

So, we started talking about what would attract really great engineers. It turns out many of them want a couple of things. Firstly, they really like tough engineering problems. They don't like the easy stuff, because it's boring. And, secondly, they want to make things that have a purpose and make a difference.

I said to the Managing Director, "As I remember it, the equipment you make saves lives. And you take on the projects that your competitors turn away because they think they're impossible."

"That's right", he replied, "The daft thing is, we've never shared any of this in the job adverts."

Unsurprisingly, when they started to tell the world that's what they did, they saw an influx of really strong candidates. The very next person they hired was a senior software engineer at Microsoft. In the Managing Director's words, "We had no right to recruit this guy. He should be out of our league." Interestingly, he left a job that was on his doorstep and chose a 90 minute commute every day.

This was not an isolated example either. They recruited a raft of great people that chose to leave jobs at multinational corporations, just a few minutes from their homes, to join this small business in a market town on the edge of the moors.

So, how can you create this magnetism?

Before answering that question, it's probably worth highlighting the two elements of magnetism.

Role Magnetism.

Why would a great candidate want to do this job?

Organisational Magnetism.

Why would they want to work here, with us?

WHY WOULD A GREAT CANDIDATE WANT TO DO THIS ROLE?	WHY WOULD THEY WANT TO WORK HERE, WITH US?

CHAPTER NINE

How can we communicate this?

Have you ever seen the famous advert that Ernest Shackleton reputedly posted when he was recruiting for his Antarctic expedition in 1907?

It says, "Men wanted for hazardous journey. Low wages, bitter cold, long hours of complete darkness. Safe return doubtful. Honour and recognition in event of success." (Watkins, 2003.)

I suspect that most people reading that would immediately think, "That's not for me" or "That doesn't sound like much fun."

And, as far as Shackleton was concerned, that's good!

A magnet has two poles. One attracts. The other repels.

> Becoming magnetic means that we attract our
> ideal candidates and repel those who aren't.

I suspect that, rightly or wrongly, Shackleton only wanted male applicants. He also wanted those who would actively choose the kind of expedition that he was embarking on. If you seek comfort and prefer life's luxuries, this kind of mission is going to sound like hell, so you won't apply.

When we think about adverts in this way, they become the first filter in our recruitment process.

Of course, we don't just want to repel people. We also need to help our ideal candidates know why this is a place they'd love to be. Over the years I've found that blending these two elements of magnetism can be incredibly powerful. I often describe great job adverts as a combination of 'Marks & Spencer's Food meets The Royal Marines'.

If you watched adverts on UK television in the mid 2000s, you may remember the famous 'melt-in-the-middle chocolate pudding'. It told the viewer that their chocolate pudding was no ordinary chocolate pudding. It was an M&S chocolate fondant pudding with a delicious gooey, melt-in-the-mouth chocolate centre. In fact, their entire food advertising campaign revolved around the idea that this was no ordinary food, it was M&S Food.

At around the same time (mid 2000s) the Royal Marines broadcast a recruitment advert which ended with the words "99% need not apply." Like the Shackleton advert, it told the world that only the very best make it through the selection process. Only a tiny percentage would wear the fabled green beret... so there's probably no point in applying. A friend of mine was a recruitment officer in the British Armed Forces. He'd often see the dynamic at a multi-service recruitment event. He described how each of the services (Army, Navy, Air Force and Marines) would have a table. When people approached the Army, Navy and Air Force, they'd be encouraged to join and given an application form. If someone approached the Royal Marines table they'd be told, "You're probably better off applying for the Army, Navy or Air Force. They might take you, but we only take the best."

Guess who had the longest queue.

Both the M&S Food and Royal Marines messages are powerful. Imagine what would happen if we combined them.

This is no ordinary job.
We are an exceptional organisation.
We do incredible things.
We're only interested in the best.
99% need not apply.
But, if you think you have what it takes, click here.

How could you create messages that are magnetic to your ideal candidates?

THE M&S FOOD BIT...	THE ROYAL MARINES BIT...

CHAPTER TEN

How do you reach your ideal candidates?

To help answer that question, I'm going to ask a different question.

What if your ideal candidate doesn't currently work in your industry?

Do you remember me mentioning a construction company who were recruiting sales executives? When we started working together the Sales Director said, "The problem is, there just aren't that many people operating in this sector. So, when we're recruiting, we get the same people going round and round between a handful of companies. I've actually told my team to stop recruiting people who have failed here before... and definitely stop hiring people who have failed here twice before!"

So, I asked her, "Have you thought about hiring really good sales executives with no experience in your industry... or even... hiring great people with no experience in sales?"

Right at the start of this book, I differentiated between hiring people on character and hiring people on their CV. It's one thing to look beyond their CV. It's another to actively look for people who don't have the knowledge, skills or experience in your industry.

Of course, there is always a context. If you were recruiting a Consultant Cardiac Surgeon, it makes sense to consider candidates who have medical training and experience in the field. However, for many roles, we could take the blinkers off and look a little wider.

Another client of mine, who operates in the Civil Engineering business (they build bridges over railways, canals, rivers and highways), have begun to adopt this thinking. Recently, they've recruited for a couple of senior roles – an Operations Director and a Head of Engineering Assurance. In the past, they've only looked at candidates who have industry experience. As one of the Directors explained, it means that (theoretically) new recruits should be able to hit the ground running. However, theirs is a small industry. Traditionally, it is one that has been largely dominated by middle aged, white, men who have all been working to the same norms and tend to think in the same way. Like many businesses, they are keen to become more diverse, widen their skill set, bring in people with different perspectives and embrace some new thinking. A Director expressed it by saying, "We've been fishing in a small pond. To get the kind of candidates we want, we need to look in places we've not looked before." So, they expanded their search beyond their industry.

Obviously, as with any role, there will be a set of core skills that a candidate needs. To be a successful Operations Director, candidates will need to be an experienced senior leader. They will need to have built teams and led teams, managed budgets, created and executed strategies, and so on. However, the company also knew that if they hired the right person, the industry knowledge can be learned relatively quickly. Much of the industry knowledge they need already exists within the team. In fact, by appointing someone with little or no domain expertise, they're also likely to find a person who asks great questions, has very few assumptions or pre-conceived ideas and brings a fresh new perspective.

––––––––––––

If we begin to focus on the characteristics we're looking for, we can then start to ask who might have them and where we might find them.

When we were looking for sales executives who were tenacious, empathetic, and adaptable, we asked the team a few questions to get them thinking.

What kind of roles would attract this kind of person?

Which companies or organisations would also look for people with these characteristics?

When they started discussing it, they realised that there are professions that require these qualities in their people, such as airline cabin crew or retail staff that sold luxury items for luxury brands.

There are also companies – often the ones that genuinely prize customer service and customer experience – who will go out of their way to attract these kinds of people, develop them, retain them, and promote them.

When they put these two elements together, they concluded that any cabin crew leaving an airline such as Virgin Atlantic, had the potential to be great sales executives in their business. Obviously, it doesn't mean that they'll blindly offer jobs to any former Virgin cabin crew. None of this replaces the need to test people and make them demonstrate the characteristics. But it does help them understand how they might start to expand their search and reach more candidates who have the characteristics they need. Interestingly, they also asked their marketing team to position job adverts and employer brand 'in the line of sight' of these kinds of people.

I'm going to throw in a sense-check at this point.

I've spoken to lots of leaders over the years who say things like...

"I need people who are driven and determined, so I'm going to focus on recruiting former elite athletes."

or

"I'm looking for people who have discipline, so I'm going to target people as they leave the Armed Forces."

That's fine. I'm not arguing against that logic, because there's a lot in it. But, in my experience, it doesn't provide the full answer. We still need to identify the top three or four characteristics that will make someone successful (not just the headline answer of 'discipline'). And we need to test candidates to make sure they have these characteristics! It's easy to assume that if you recruit an Olympic athlete, they'll automatically be amazing at everything. I know a lot of Olympians. Some go on to have an incredible post-athletic career. Others struggle. There are many transferable skills and characteristics. But we need to make sure the candidates have them, not assume.

If you're interested in understanding this in more detail, check out *The Podium Podcast*, which focuses on how athletes translate their performance mindset into business.

You can find every episode at **beworldclass.tv**

CHAPTER ELEVEN

From Starters to Superstars.

If you remember back to the recruitment timeline, the process doesn't finish when they sign the contract of employment, walk through the door for their first day or even when they pass 'probation'. I'd argue that it extends way beyond that. The aim, as I see it, is that your new recruit goes on to become highly successful – consistently delivering high performance, developing, progressing through the organisation, and getting promoted. When we take this longer-term view, the decisions we make to retain people, invest in them, and promote them, are all recruitment decisions.

I've worked with lots of elite sports teams over the years. They understand that moving a player from the under 15s to under 17s is a recruitment decision. Some players make it. Some don't. Who gets selected? Who doesn't?

In the same way, promoting people within a business and deciding who to invest in, are also recruitment decisions. Therefore, I'd argue that recruitment is a seamless, on going process that extends through their induction and probation period (if you have one), through on going PDPs (Personal Development Plans), performance reviews, appraisals, etc. Arguably, it should be a spine that supports them throughout their time with your organisation.

So, what happens once we've made someone an offer?

What's the next step?

Interestingly, I've noticed that even world-class teams and organisations, who have an incredibly robust recruitment process, don't always get it right. Sometimes they make mistakes too. And, whilst they might not get every hire right, they are very good at noticing early and acting when they miss the mark. Often this means that they 'de-select' people (say goodbye) within three to four weeks if they're not the right person.

When I share this with business leaders, I often see some raised eyebrows and here questions like...

"A few weeks? Really? Not months?"

I've noticed that they're able to do this because they 'get their eye in' as I describe it. Simply, this means that they keep looking at how people demonstrate their critical characteristics past the point at which they make an offer.

We humans can put up a façade for a while. For example, we can get dressed up and put our best game-face on for a few hours during an interview or an assessment centre. In fact, some people are very good at presenting themselves. They can look the part and talk a great game – sales people can be particularly good at this. But what they present at interview may not be the 'real person'. And, whilst we humans can project a façade for a few hours or a few days, eventually our guard drops, and we show our true colours. Of course, this is what world-class organisations are looking for.

I've asked the very best leaders what they look for and listen for during these first few weeks. It often starts as they make a job offer and begin discussing the details of a contract. For example, does the candidate ask how many holiday days they are entitled to, which car parking space they'll get, which office they'll be given, or the benefits package? Are the early conversations geared around what they'll get? If so, the alarm bells might start ringing.

When I've shared the concept of 'de-selecting early' with Sales Directors and Sales Managers, many will say, "We have to give a person long enough to deliver some results. That might take months." In fact, one Sales Director told me he'd had a sales executive in the business for almost a year, with zero sales, because "they always seemed to have this 'huge deal' that was just about to land."

I don't disagree that it could take months to see results. However, I would argue that we don't need to wait for results. If we look at the processes (i.e., what people are doing and how well they're doing it), we will see whether they're likely to get the results or not. And, if we get our eye in, we'll also be able to see whether they're displaying and developing the characteristics we need. If they are... it's a good sign they have a promising future. If not, it might be worth taking a step back and reviewing.

Making this kind of call after just a few weeks is a bold decision, I know. However, in my experience, it's the fairest course of action for everyone concerned. If the person is the wrong fit, it will probably have a negative impact on the organisation and the team. One of the early questions in this book asked, "What's the cost of hiring the wrong people?" As you might remember, there are multiple layers to this – team morale, the costs of investment, training, salary, reputation, etc. These can be significant, especially if we keep people who aren't a good fit.

However, there is another element, which sometimes gets missed. I've also learned that keeping a new recruit who isn't quite right is unfair to them. Ultimately, if they're not a good fit for the organisation or the role, they'll struggle. No one likes to struggle in their role. Our human tendency, if we feel out of our depth, is to hide it, cover up mistakes, deflect attention, become defensive, make excuses, blame others, etc. All of this takes a lot of mental and emotional effort. It becomes tiring. It normally creates anxiety and makes people miserable. And, whilst they may not thank you for making the decision in the short term, I suspect they will in the long term.

How do we know whether our new recruit is a good fit?

World-class organisations work on the principle that no one is the finished article. Everyone has scope to grow and improve. Therefore, from day one, they test whether their new recruit has the appetite and ability to develop these critical characteristics. In essence, the character tests they employ during the recruitment process provide an initial assessment. It shows how strongly each candidate displays the characteristics they need. If we used a simple 0-10 scoring system for each characteristic (where 0 means 'nothing good whatsoever' and 10 means 'perfect, flawless and can't be improved') we'll find that even the best candidates don't score 10. Therefore, there's always headroom to grow into. So, world-class organisations start challenging new recruits to develop these from day one. If they see progress, it's a good sign that they've recruited well. If they don't see progress, it's probably wise to ask whether their new recruit is a good fit or not.

I often use a simple staircase model to develop characteristics. These staircases are built on the understanding that we're not asking people to leap to the top of the staircase. If they're currently on the second step, we're challenging them to get to the third. Once they've consistently nailed the third step, we can challenge them to get to the fourth. And, as long as they keep climbing, they will continue to develop.

Here are a couple of examples that I included in *How to Develop Character* (Hartley, 2015).

Be Passionate

They create a culture of pride within their own team and nuture pride in others.

They seek their discomfort zone and invite critical feedback to help them improve what they do because it matters to them.

They consistently do what it takes to get the job done well and take real pride in it.

Leaders are happy and willing to take on tougher challenges that demand more of them and greater commitment.

Leaders tell you what they're proud about and committed to through daily conversations.

Be The Solution

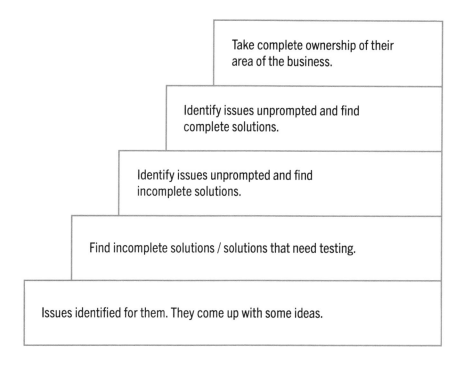

Take complete ownership of their area of the business.

Identify issues unprompted and find complete solutions.

Identify issues unprompted and find incomplete solutions.

Find incomplete solutions / solutions that need testing.

Issues identified for them. They come up with some ideas.

Of course, it's important to marry challenge with support. Over the decades, I've found that a balance between challenge and support is critical if we want people to grow and develop.

> As the level of challenge increases, so should the level of support. But it's always grounded in the principle that everyone is responsible for their own development.

We can support them, but we can't do it for them. Ultimately, their response to the challenges will tell us whether they've got the stuff we're looking for or not.

CHAPTER TWELVE

How do we build a pathway to excellence?

When I look at most organisations, I see a pattern. If you want to progress in your career, you need to become a manager. It's the way most corporate structures are created. Often people come in 'at the bottom'. And, over time, they progress to a junior management position, through middle management and towards senior management. As people walk this path, they get fancier job titles and increases in salary. The whole system seems to be built on the basis that progression and management go hand in hand.

Now, I'm not saying that the system is wrong or that it should be scrapped. However, I would question whether it's the only way. I'd also question whether a different approach might work better in some situations. I've lost count of the times I've heard the phrase, "They were a wonderful Sales Executive, so the company promoted them to become the Sales Manager and it was a disaster." During my time in professional sport, I've also seen great players who really struggled when they were given the captaincy, or a coaching or management role. Of course, the fact that someone is a good Sales Executive or a good sports player, doesn't automatically give them the skills, aptitude, or desire to be a great manager. Leadership is a very different skill set. However, if that's the only progression route on offer, we may force people down a path that draws on their weaknesses, rather than their strengths.

Earlier, I mentioned an engineering business that were looking to recruit 'Sherlock'. Because they had a clear idea of the characteristics they needed, and how to test for them, they found their man. As Paul, who recruited for the role said, "He was a perfect fit for the role." In fact, he was so good, they promoted him into a management role. If you've ever watched (or read) Sherlock Holmes, you'll realise that Sherlock is a sociopath. He is technically amazing, but people skills are not his strength.

It probably won't surprise you to know that our 'Sherlock' struggled in his management role too. Fortunately, the business realised their error and gave him a progression route that allowed him to become a better technical expert, rather than forcing him into management.

> Many of the great organisations I've encountered recognise the importance of multiple progression routes. The most common two are 'management' and 'mastery'.

The mastery route enables people to gain those fancier job titles and higher salaries, without taking on management responsibilities. It recognises that by becoming better in their field – engineering, sales, surgery, teaching, or whatever it is – they become more valuable to the organisation. The organisation therefore starts to invest in developing mastery and recognising people for it. And, whilst these technical masters can pass on their expertise to others (maybe through mentoring), the organisation doesn't ask them to play out-of-position by managing people.

13

CHAPTER THIRTEEN

None of this will happen without...
Great Leadership.

I know this is going to sound blindingly obvious, but if you recruit great people into a team with a terrible leader, they're not going to hang around for long. And whilst it sounds almost too obvious to mention, I've seen multiple organisations get this wrong.

You can probably see how this unravels. Great people can be more challenging. They'll ask questions, like, "Why do we do it like that?" and "How can we do this better?" They'll often push standards. They'll identify opportunities to improve and have a strong desire to drive performance. They tend to demand more from those around them. And whilst these are incredibly valuable qualities, they can make some people feel uncomfortable... or even threatened. I've seen some managers become defensive and controlling because they feel under threat. Rather than giving their people license to perform, insecure managers will often grip the reins even tighter. Great people seek autonomy and responsibility, not micro-management. So, when these issues start to compound, it can create real problems.

On reflection, organisations don't deliberately shoot themselves in the foot. They don't march into the process knowing that their leaders are below par. But they often go in hoping that they'll be good enough. They hope their leaders will welcome the challenge and embrace it. They hope that their leader will get the best out of these wonderful new recruits.

In my experience, hope is not a strategy. I'd also say that hope is a pretty weak expression of confidence. When I was working in the Olympic programmes, I created a Confidence Scale. I'd chat with the athletes a few weeks before a competition and ask how confident they were feeling. I noticed that their answers varied from "I hope I'll do okay" to "I know I'm going to do well."

| Hope | Think | Confident that... | Believe | Know |

The same scale can be used to assess our own confidence in all kinds of areas. For example...

How confident are you that...

... this person is right for your organisation?

... they'll be successful in this role?

... your leaders will welcome the challenge that really good new recruits will bring?

However confident the athletes in the Olympic programmes were (whether they said, "I hope" or "I believe"), my next questions were... "How can we get you as close to saying 'I know' as possible, by competition day? What can we do to move you closer to 'I know'?"

This tends to highlight the gaps and give us some ideas on how to bridge them.

———————

I guess that's a long-winded way of making a simple point.

Before diving in to recruit great people, it's worth reflecting on the strength of leadership in your organisation and how to develop it.

14

CHAPTER FOURTEEN

—

Time to pull all of this together.

To help you put all of this into action, here's a quick summary of the key points.

———

Firstly...

Like many things, hiring great people is simple but not easy. Recruiting on character requires more time, effort, thinking and energy (although it doesn't usually require a huge amount more cash). So, we need to know that extra investment is worth it.

At the start of this book, I asked a couple of key questions...

What's the benefit of getting recruitment right?

What's the cost if we don't?

I've shared some research (such as Paul Stoltz's findings) and some examples from my clients. But ultimately, you need to know the difference it makes to you, and your organisation.

Secondly...

Once we've done that, we can start identifying the characteristics we really need in our people. Obviously, we're talking about characteristics here, not personality. There will be common characteristics we want in everyone – I call these Organisational Characteristics. These characteristics will often be the embodiment of our values and live at the heart of our culture. And, there will be some characteristics that are vital for someone to be successful in their role – I call these Role Characteristics.

The trap many fall into, is to describe a super-human. Of course, we're unlikely to find anyone matching that description. So, we need to narrow down to a handful of critical characteristics. I find it helps to put these in rank order so that we all know which are most important and why. We also need a common understanding of these characteristics. When we say, 'honesty', what do we mean? Are we saying that we want people who have never lied (ever), or do we mean something else?

Once we have identified the characteristics, we can build the other pieces of the jigsaw.

We can start to create the tests that we'll use and build them into our recruitment timeline. Critically, these tests make people demonstrate the characteristics we're looking for (not tell us about them). It often helps to stretch our minds by adopting '11 star thinking'. It also helps to use real-life challenges that our people have encountered.

I've shared some examples of how other organisations approach this. It's great to see how world-class teams such as the Red Arrows or Special Forces units do it. It's also interesting to see how a primary school did it. But ultimately the tests have to work for you in your context. By sharing these examples, my intention is to spark your thinking, rather than give you 'cut and paste' tests.

It's often worth validating your tests on your current team. We should find that our best people perform better in the tests. If not, it's worth having a rethink before rolling them out.

Experience tells me that we will probably have a few iterations before we settle on a process we're happy with, and have confidence in. I advise my clients to embrace the principle of 'Plan – Do – Review – Adapt – Go Again'. Most find that they're happy with their second or third iteration.

Knowing that this will be an attritional process, we also need to become a magnet for talent. I describe two kinds of magnetism – organisational magnetism and role magnetism. To develop these, we need to be able to answer a few critical questions.

Why would our ideal candidate want to work here (with us)?

Why would they want to do this role?

How do we create a queue outside the door?

Getting our marketing messages and job adverts right is one element of this. But it's not the whole picture. Our ideal candidates need more than a good job advert. Our organisation needs to become the place where great people want to work. Building this magnetism can take a while. It's not going to happen overnight. Equally, it's not 'all or nothing'. It's often a case of building on what we already have, consistently, over a long period.

And finally...

The recruitment process doesn't end once we've made an offer. Great organisations 'get their eye in' early, so that they learn about the person beyond the interview. They know that no one is the finished article, so world-class organisations start challenging and supporting their new recruits to keep developing the critical characteristics. It forms part of a seamless development process from recruitment, through induction and 'probation', into ongoing PDPs, performance reviews and promotions.

To get the very best from their people, I've found that great organisations also ensure there are a variety of ways to progress – not just management!

And, to reinforce the obvious point... None of this can happen without good leadership!

———————

As I said... It's simple, but not necessarily easy.

The upside, of course, is that hiring great people has a huge positive impact on any organisation. Or, as a friend of mine once said...

"Great teams are founded on great people."

Thank you for reading Hire Great People.
I hope you enjoyed it. Please enjoy an excerpt from
my seventh book *How To Develop Character*.

HOW TO DEVELOP CHARACTER

Chapter 1 - What is Character?

A person's character helps to define them. It helps us to understand them as an individual.

In psychology, there are several ways to understand people's individuality and uniqueness. One is personality. This has been described as the combination of qualities that make an individual distinct. When differentiating personalities, psychologists look for the patterns of thoughts, feelings and behaviours. For example, there are differences in the way that people make decisions and solve problems. Some people are goal-driven and decisive. Others will seek to involve others and gain consensus when making decisions. Some are analytical and able to process the tiny details. Others are more creative and conceptual; the 'lateral' thinkers. By discovering our personality and our tendencies, we can begin to understand how we think, solve problems, communicate and how we're motivated. Whilst this is very useful, it doesn't tell us about our character.

Character goes beyond personality. Equally, it goes beyond both skills and knowledge. Skill is often defined as our learned ability to execute a task and bring about a pre-determined outcome. It is commonly described as 'a learned activity'. Throwing a ball, reading, and riding a bicycle are classic examples of skills that we learn. As we improve skills, we tend to become more accurate, precise, consistent and efficient. However, our level of skill does not necessarily inform us about our character. The same is true of knowledge. Knowledge tends to be thought of as the acquisition of facts and information through experience and education. Therefore character and knowledge may not be related either. Merely acquiring skills or knowledge doesn't help us develop character. As John Corlett states, "virtues are, in contrast, not masteries of technique; technique has very little to do with being brave, generous or honest; nor do these necessarily involve being proficient at any particular thing."

So, if character is not just the combination of our skills, knowledge and personality, what is it?

I see character almost as our 'personal culture'. Culture, of course, relates to groups of people. The culture within a team, organisation or society reflects its shared values and beliefs. Personally, I describe culture by saying "it's what we say and do on a daily basis." If our character is akin to personal or individual culture, I might describe it using the phrase, "it's what I say and do on a daily basis." It is the outward expression of who I am. It is the way I live my personal qualities, values, beliefs and philosophy.

Abraham Lincoln said, "Reputation is the shadow. Character is the tree."

The Oxford Dictionary defined character as, "The mental and moral qualities distinctive to an individual."

Tom Hill describes it as, "The qualities built into an individual's life that determine his or her response, regardless of circumstances." He likens it to a moral compass and the ability to follow our conscience.

"The measure of a man's character is what he would do if he knew he would never be found out", Baron Thomas Babington Macauley.

Importantly, character has more than just a mental dimension. It also has a moral dimension. As Josef Pieper says, our character underpins our ability to do the right thing for the right reasons. It drives who we are and what we do when no one is watching. It shapes how we respond to situations regardless of the circumstances or the likely outcomes. An honest and truthful person will not decide whether to lie or not, depending on the likely outcome. They will be truthful because it is right to do so. Marvin Berkowitz, Professor of Character Education at the University of Missouri, describes character as, "the set of psychological characteristics that motivate and enable the individual to function as a competent moral agent; that is 'to do good in the world.'"

The distinctions between skills, knowledge, personality and character are not merely academic. They have real significance for those who seek to develop character. It means that character cannot be developed in the same way as skills and knowledge, or formed in the same way as personality.

Purchase *How To Develop Character*

Amazon UK
amazon.co.uk/dp/B01C4ELVKM

Amazon USA
amazon.com/dp/B01C4ELVKM

To find out more about my work
and my other books please visit:
be-world-class.com

BIBLIOGRAPHY

Devaney, J. (1967) Bart Starr, New York: Scholastic Book Services.

Elite UK Forces (2023) 'Special Air Service Selection / How to Join'. [available online https://www.eliteukforces.info/special-air-service/sas-selection/]

Gallagher, L. (2017) *The Airbnb Story: How three ordinary guys disrupted an industry, made billions... and created plenty of controversy.* New York: Harper Business Press.

Hartley, S. R. (2012) *How to Shine; Insights into unlocking your potential from proven winners*, Chichester: Capstone.

Hartley, S. R. (2015) *Stronger Together; How great teams work*, London: Piatkus.

Hartley, S. R. (2015) *How to Develop Character*, Leeds: Be World Class.

Hartley, S. R. (2018) *Master Mental Toughness*, Leeds: Be World Class.

Hayes, A. (2021) 'This is what it takes to join the SAS', Men's Health. May 2021 [available online https://www.menshealth.com/uk/fitness/a36379046/sas-training-selection/]

Hill, T. (2010) *Making Character First*, Oklahoma City: Character First Publishers.

Kerr, J. (2013) *Legacy; What the All Blacks Can Teach Us About The Business Of Life*. London: Constable.

Stoltz, P. (2015) *GRIT: The New Science of What It Takes to Persevere, Flourish, Succeed*. San Luis Obispo, CA: Climb Strong Press.

Watkins, J. L. (2003) *100 Greatest Advertisements 1852-1958; Who wrote them and what they did*, Mineola, NY: Dover Publications.

Willink, J. and Babin, L. (2015) *Extreme Ownership; How US Navy SEALs Lead and Win*, New York: St Martin's Press.

ABOUT SIMON HARTLEY

Hi, I'm Simon.

I'm passionate about helping individuals, teams, leaders and organisations unlock their potential and become world-class in their field!

My background is sport psychology. I've spent much of my career working with elite athletes and sports teams, helping them to get their mental game and their mindset right.

But my real passion is working with and studying the very best in the world. I love figuring out what makes them great and then helping others adopt those principles.

Over the years, I've written a few non-fiction books, to share what I've learned about mindset, teams, leadership, and world-class performance. I also wrote a fictional book, called *Silence Your Demons*, to help people navigate mental and emotional challenges.

I share these lessons through my coaching, podcasts and speaking work, and through a few digital programmes.

If you fancy finding out more, feel free to check out my other books.

... and visit the Be World Class website for more.

be-world-class.com

OTHER BOOKS BY SIMON HARTLEY

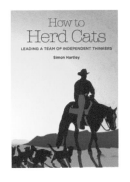